## SERMON OUTLINES
### on

# Great Themes of the Bible

## Charles R. Wood

PUBLICATIONS

Grand Rapids, MI 49501

*Sermon Outlines on Great Themes of the Bible*
by Charles R. Wood

© 1991 by Kregel Publications, a division of Kregel, Inc.,
P.O. Box 2607, Grand Rapids, MI 49501.

All rights reserved. No part of this book may be repro-
duced, stored in a retrieval system, or transmitted in any
form or by any means—electronic, mechanical, photo-
copy, recording, or otherwise—without written permis-
sion of the publisher, except for brief quotations in printed
reviews.

For more information about Kregel Publications, visit our
web site at: www.kregel.com

**Library of Congress Cataloging-in-Publication**
Sermon outlines on great themes of the Bible / by Charles
R. Wood.
      p.      cm.
1. Sermons—Outlines, syllabi, etc. I. Title.
BV4223.W663   1991                91-27157
252'.02—dc20

ISBN 0-8254-4133-1

3  4  5  6  7  printing / year  04  03  02  01  00

*Printed in the United States of America*

## Introduction

The Bible is an amazing Book! A lifetime of study fails to exhaust its treasures and leaves one feeling that there is more potential for exploration than one could hope to work through in another lifetime.

Great, dominating themes abound in this God-breathed Book, and many of them have marched forth from the pages of Scripture to become central factors in the growth and structure of Christianity. Sin, salvation, regneration, sanctification, confession, forgiveness, heaven, hell, and a host of other themes not only occupy center stage in the Word of God but spill over into the everyday lives of God's people. We are often consumed by questions which deal with these themes and plagued by lack of more precise knowledge regarding their actual meanings and applications.

The sermons in this book represent one preacher's attempt to deal with these biblical themes, both defining precisely the issues which they encompass and expressing clearly the implications they present. The major issues of biblical concern are treated here along with some of those which are less commonly stressed. The outlines are the distilled result of careful exegesis, diligent regard to principles of biblical interpretation, and thoughtful comparisons with the results of the scholarship of others.

Although the outlines are original, there is no claim to originality of thought or interpretation. If it is true that we are the sum total of the influences to which we have been subjected throughout our lives, it is inevitable that one who has studied under outstanding scholars and read widely in the "masters" will reveal those influences in his own work.

As is the case with every book of sermon outlines in this series, these messages are not designed to be taken directly from the book into the pulpit. They will be most beneficial both to the preacher and to his congregation if they are first used as study guides to the passages they treat. Once one has spent adequate time in Bible study, the outlines will then also function in assisting the organization of the presentation of the results of such study. There is one complaint coming from the pew today that is heard more than any other. It has to do with the fact that so many pulpit presentations are either unorganized or disorganized. If these outlines do nothing else, they should help in the organization of the material to be presented.

These are not "literary" sermons. They were prepared to be

preached, and they have all been preached by the editor in the pulpit of the local church of which he is pastor. Most of them have been preached within a relatively brief period of time prior to their publication as part of this series.

These messages are presented in the hope that they will make the themes of Scripture live in the minds of preachers and congregations alike, both by suggesting clear and precise definitions of those themes and also by providing practical ways in which those themes can be related to the everyday lives of God's people. May the Holy Spirit who empowered their original preparation also guide their representation to usefulness in His service.

# Contents

# Textual Index

# The Justice of God

## Genesis 3

**Introduction:**

God frequently met with men in Scripture. This is especially true in the Old Testament. We learn much about God from these encounters. From this particular encounter we can learn the great truth of God's justice.

I. **Justice Is Always Based on Individual Responsibility**
   A. Adam and Eve use a "blameshift" defense
   B. God completely ignores that defense
   C. God deals with each individual as if each were totally to blame
      1. Blame is often shared
      2. Blame can never be shifted

II. **Justice Always Does What Is Promised or Threatened**
   A. God, indeed, had spoken
   B. The prohibition was "in the day that thou doest it, thou shalt begin to die"
   C. That was exactly what happened
      1. God did not fail to follow through
      2. When there is such failure, it always leads to problems

III. **Justice Always Suits the Punishment to the Crime**
   A. Each was dealt with individually
   B. Each received punishment worthy of his crime, no more nor less
   C. Real justice always involves balance

IV. **Justice Always Mixes Mercy With Judgment**
   A. God's judgment always includes mercy
      1. Even Satan received a measure of mercy
      2. The man and the woman found mercy
      3. Mercy is seen in clothing them with skins
   B. We are far wiser to operate on mercy than on judgment
      1. Don't ask for what you have coming from God as you may get it
      2. Chastisement is justice, repentance calls on mercy
      3. Thus it is merciful to call sin by its real name

**Conclusion:**

The justice of God is nothing to fool with. A man is a fool to fool with it. "Yea, hath God said?"

# Sin

## Genesis 39:9

**Introduction:**

The story of Joseph is extraordinary. Just when it appeared he was "turning it around," a woman sought to seduce him. He asks a burning question, "How then can I do this great wickedness and sin against God?" The only way men can sin in such ways is:

**I.   By Taking a Low View of Sin**
   A.   Sin is not serious
   B.   Sin is just natural to man
   C.   Other people are doing this
   D.   My sin is no worse than any other

**II.   By Taking a Casual View of God's Justice**
   A.   God can't do anything about it
   B.   God won't do anything about it
   C.   God hasn't done anything about it
   D.   God doesn't do anything about these things

**III.   By Taking an Exalted View of One's Importance**
   A.   I don't live by the rules for others
   B.   I am specially valuable to God
   C.   What satisfies me is what is most significant
   D.   I go by what makes me feel important

**IV.   By Taking an Indifferent View of the Well-Being of Others**
   A.   I am unaware of the effects of my sin
   B.   I don't care about the effects of my sin
   C.   I want my own way badly enough to make it worthwhile to ruin others
   D.   I have no concern for the well-being of others

**Conclusion:**

Joseph rejected all these approaches and thus resisted sin. Our rejection of this thinking could keep us from sin. We have much to learn from Joseph!

# The Mercy of God

## Deuteronomy 4:29-34

**Introduction:**

What is the most dominant characteristic in God? Sometimes I think it must be patience. It is clearly shown here. This passage deals with patience as it relates to the subjects of backsliding and revival.

I. **The Reason for Revival—Backsliding (29)**
   - A. "If from thence" (cf. vs. 25-28)
   - B. This illustrates Proverbs 14:14
   - C. The danger:
     1. Not all backsliding ends up with obvious trouble
     2. Some does end up thus
     3. Much of God's recompense is very gradual or imperceptible

II. **The Reach of Revival (29-30)**
   - A. From any place of trouble
     1. "When thou art in tribulation"
     2. God often uses troubles to get our attention
   - B. "When all these things have happened . . ."
     1. When you have failed to heed
     2. When you end up in a "worst case" scenario
   - C. Even in the latter days
     1. This can mean "last days"
     2. This can also mean "even after a long time away"

III. **The Recipe for Revival (29)**
   - A. Seek the Lord: turn back to Him
   - B. Seek Him wholeheartedly
   - C. Be obedient unto His voice
     1. No stress on sorrow as repentance is not just feeling sorry
     2. Obedience to the Word plays a part
   - D. Actually this is a very simple process that we complicate

IV. **The Reality of Revival (32-34)**
   - A. God is merciful; He is looking for ways to bless and avoid punishing
   - B. God loves His people
     1. He has shown it historically
     2. He has shown it in our lives
   - C. God is faithful to His covenant obligations
     1. He had a covenant with Israel
     2. He has a covenant with us

**Conclusion:**

Israel went away from God, lured by the nations about them. They ended up filled with their desired ways (they got what they wanted, but they didn't want what they got). God says, "When you get to that place, remember what you had, remember how you had been treated, but also beware of My judgment."

# The Anger of God

### Psalm 7:11

**Introduction:**

Is it ever right to get angry? Obviously it is. There are three guidelines:

Over a sufficient cause

With a proportional reaction

For a properly limited period of time

We know it is right because God gets angry, and here's proof

I. **The Prominence of the Theme**
   A. We usually think of God in terms of love
   B. There are more references to the anger of God than to the love of God
      1. Main passages: Nahum 1:2-8; 2 Thessalonians 1:8ff.
      2. A recurring theme in Romans:1:18; 2:5; 5:9; 12:19; 13:4ff.

II. **The Problem of the Theme**
   A. Because we think God is like us rather than we like Him, this concept troubles us
      1. Most human anger is not righteous
      2. Thus, we think of anger as a negative that really can't be right
   B. God's anger is logical
      1. Would a God who took as much pleasure in evil as in good make any sense?
      2. Would a universe where good went unrewarded and evil unpunished be rational?
   C. Logic and reason (patterned after God's) demand an angry side to God

III. **The Particulars of the Theme**
   A. God's wrath is judicial
      1. It is part of God's resolute action in punishing sin
      2. There is no passion, personal frustration, in it at all
      3. It is strictly a manifestation of God's justice
   B. God's wrath is retributive (Romans 2:5)
      1. God is never angry without a cause
      2. Man gets what he deserves
   C. God's wrath is proportional (Luke 12:47)
      1. Man gets exactly what he deserves
      2. God measures out His wrath with precision
   D. God's wrath is continual (Romans 1:18)
      1. God is right now exercising His wrath

        2. Events in this world indicate what the wrath of God is like

   E. God's wrath is chosen (John 3:18)

        1. Men call it down upon themselves by retreating from light

        2. God gives men what they choose

        3. God ratifies and confirms the judgments which men pass on themselves by the courses they follow

## IV. The Pertinence of the Theme

   A. God's wrath is necessary to make sense of the Gospel, the Bible, and the world

   B. God's wrath

        1. Shows us God's detestation of sin

        2. Gives birth in our souls to a proper fear of God

        3. Should make us praise Him for delivering us from wrath

## Conclusion:

The most important issue is the certainty that we have escaped from the wrath of God through Christ (Romans 5:9)

# *Prayer*

### Psalm 66:18

**Introduction:**
God always answers prayer, but sometimes He says "yes," and sometimes He says "no." At other times He says, "not yet." God always has purposes for what He does. It is possible some "no" or "later" answers could be turned into immediate "yes" answers. We often fail to get what we seek because of defective prayer. There are three primary problems.

I. **Self-Centeredness (James 4:3)**
   A. Some element of God's glory must be present
      1. God has nothing to do with some men's success
      2. Why ask God to prosper you when you have no intention of sharing that prosperity with Him?
   B. God doesn't answer when our prayer is aimed at wasteful results
   C. God may not answer demanding prayer

II. **Bitterness (Matthew 5:23 & 24, 6:12,14 & 15; 1 Peter 3:7 with Colossians 3:19)**
   A. Any bitterness will block answers
   B. The highest price for bitterness is always paid by the one who is bitter
      1. The other person often doesn't even know it
      2. Power in prayer is thus lost
   C. Bitterness often has a strong measure of self-righteousness in it
      1. "I am right; others wrong"
      2. A heart full of bitterness can't offer a proper prayer

III. **Alliance With Sin (Psalm 26:18)**
   A. The secret practice of sin
      1. Passage deals with known sin
      2. It does not have to be in the moral realm
   B. Entertaining sin which includes desire to commit it
      1. It is no sin to be tempted
      2. Sin comes when we entertain temptation
   C. Reflecting on sin with delight
      1. Pleasureable memories
      2. Fantasizing
   D. Looking approvingly at the sins of others
      1. There is wrong in most of society (Romans 1:32)
      2. We often approve of the sins of others because they make ours a bit more palatable

E.  Unwillingness to open all areas of life to His scrutiny

**Conclusion:**

These things probably cause many "no" and "later" answers. If God were to give us what we want while we are in these states, it would encourage us to continue in them. It is time to stop questioning God and to begin examining ourselves.

# Riches

### Proverbs 23:4 & 5

**Introduction:**
How many would bring someone to church for $1,000? How many would do their present jobs for nothing? We live in a world dominated by money and its concerns. It has enormous power in our lives.

I.   **The Prohibition Regarding Riches**
   A.   The passage doesn't say, "labor not"
   B.   The passage does say, "Labor not to be rich"
      1.   The purpose of labor should not be riches (amassing money)
      2.   God has another motivation in view
   C.   "Cease from your own wisdom," no matter what you feel or hear
   D.   The reasons given
      1.   Riches take their flight
      2.   Riches really aren't anything lasting

II.   **The Problems Regarding Riches**

| Psalm 62:10 | Jeremiah 9:23 | Luke 12:15 |
|---|---|---|
| Proverbs 22:16 | Ezekiel 28:5 | 1 Timothy 6:9 & 10 |
| Proverbs 11:4 | Matthew 13:22 | 1 Timothy 6:17 |
| Proverbs 28:11 | Mark 4:19 | James 1:10 |
| Ecclesiastes 5:13 | Luke 8:14 | James 5:1 & 2 |

III.   **The Plan Regarding Riches**
   A.   Labor is part of God's plan, not part of man's fall
   B.   The fall merely made labor harder
   C.   This raises interesting points
      1.   Is there an automatic age point at which we should quit?
      2.   Is it right not to work at all?

IV.   **The Purpose of Riches**
   A.   We should labor to have riches so we can give to others (Ephesians 4:28)
   B.   We should view riches as a by-product of diligence (Proverbs 10:4)
   C.   We should strive to be "rich toward God" (Luke 12:21)
      1.   This ties in with "seek ye first"
      2.   Any labor that pulls us away from that goal is questionable

**Conclusion:**
We need to weigh our work. We need to weigh our motive for working. We need to weigh what we do with what we earn. Labor not to be rich!!!

# *Tithing*

## Malachi 3:7-15

**Introduction:**

Have you stopped beating your wife? Strongly stated questions capture attention. That's the approach of Malachi. We deal with one of those questions here.

I.   **The Controversy (7)**
  A.  Backsliding
  B.  Backsliding against grace
  C.  Refusal to admit backsliding

II.  **The Condemnation (8) "Yet ye have robbed me"**
  A.  They have robbed God (either by taking or withholding what was not theirs)
  B.  Notice tithes and offering
  C.  Consider:
    1.  These are unnatural actions that the heathen do not do
    2.  These are daring actions when we claim a living God
    3.  These are ungrateful actions
    4.  These are injurious actions
    5.  These are judged actions

III. **The Curse (9-12) "Ye are cursed with a curse"**
  A.  There is no meat in God's house. This was a disgrace
  B.  There was lack of abundance
  C.  The devourer was in operation
  D.  The fruit was spoiling before its time
  E.  The nations were wondering what was going on

IV.  **The Challenge (10) "Prove me now"**
  A.  "Bring ye all the tithes"
    1.  This would include offerings
    2.  Note the stress on all the tithes
  B.  "Into the storehouse"
    1.  The stress is not on place
    2.  Bring everything to Him
  C.  "And prove me now"
    1.  A challenge and invitation are offered instead of punishment
    2.  He puts the onus back on Himself
    3.  He includes a promise of forgiveness
  D.  "Herewith"—in this way

## V. The Commitment (10-12) "I will pour you out"
A. I will open the windows of heaven
B. I will pour you out a blessing
1. It will overflow
2. Your ability to contain it will determine the extent of it
C. I will rebuke or stay the devourer
D. Your vines will not cast early
E. All nations shall call you blessed

## Conclusion:
Malachi gets very personal and specific. If you would not take money from an offering plate, why will you fail to put money in it?

## *Priorities*

### Matthew 6:19-34

**Introduction:**

We value many things highly: family, job, career, and possessions. We don't often do very well with God's order.

I. **The Core of the Commandment**
   A. The kingdom of God
      1. The rule and reign of God
      2. The place where God is in control
   B. His righteousness
      1. Not His saving power
      2. Rather, all the rightness connected with Him

II. **The Challenge of the Commandment**
   A. "Seek ye"
      1. A word of command
      2. It means "to go after"
   B. "First"
      1. In chronology—before seeking anything else
      2. In priority—in preference to anything else
      3. In importance—as of higher good than anything else

III. **The Context of the Commandment**
   It goes back to verse 19 and contains four tremendous principles
   A. "Where your treasure . . ."
      1. What you treasure, you seek
      2. What you seek, you treasure
   B. "No man can serve two masters . . ."
      1. This has to do with a slave economy
      2. We can't be slaves to two. We are to be God's slave
   C. "For your heavenly Father knoweth . . ."
   D. "Sufficient unto the day . . ."

IV. **The Consequences of the Commandment**
   A. "All these things"
      1. The things we normally worry about
      2. The things mentioned in the passage
   B. "Shall be added unto you"
      1. You will have them
      2. You aren't solely responsible to secure them as God gives them

V. **The Conflict of the Commandment**
   A. This runs absolutely counter to our personal experience

1. We seek material things first
2. We next seek the jobs and money that care for the material concerns
3. We then seek His kingdom with what is left after all the rest is spent

B. God wants His people to see things right side up because the world sees them as upside down

## Conclusion:

We must ask proper questions such as: Am I seeking His kingdom and righteousness? How will this affect my family's spiritual dimension? How will this advance God's kingdom?

# The Golden Rule

## Matthew 7:12

**Introduction:**

A Gentile, tired of repetitions of the law, asked Rabbi Hillel to summarize the law in the length of time he could stand on one leg. Hillel said, "What is hateful to you, do not do to anyone else." That wasn't the "golden rule," but it was like it. It is also an indication that God wrote it in the hearts of all men.

I.  **The Content of the Rule**
   A.  Christ took it from negative to positive
      1.  The Jews said, "Don't do what you don't want done"
      2.  Christ said, "Do what you would have done" ("Frigid negatives satisfy neither the law nor the prophets.")
   B.  It deals with an attitude more than with actions
      1.  It is the first rule of Christian conduct
      2.  It is the law of our Lord's life
      3.  He demonstrates for us its possibility by keeping it

II.  **The Correction of the Rule**
   A.  It is not a summary of Old Testament righteousness
      1.  No one was ever saved this way
      2.  "For this sums up the law and the prophets." It is a summary of the Old Testament teaching of the law and prophets
      3.  This is right living not righteousness
   B.  It is not a utilitarian maxim
      1.  It is not to be done for what it can do for us
      2.  It is to be done because it is God's will for us
   C.  It is not the rule for mankind in general
   D.  It is not the way to secure salvation

III.  **The Caution of the Rule**
   A.  The rule of legitimacy comes into play: It must accord with the rest of Scripture
   B.  It only covers life in its relationship to other people

IV.  **The Contrasts of the Rule**
   A.  The natural man bases responses on what others have done
   B.  The usual man overlooks what others do
   C.  The unusual man responds in ways he would want others to respond
   D.  The unique man aggressively seeks opportunities to do good unto others

## V. The Challenge of the Rule
  A. The rule embraces all of life
    1. "Therefore" forms an envelope with Matthew 5:17
    2. "All things" cover everything
  B. The rule is to be followed aggressively
    1. It is not only a matter of response
    2. We also should seek opportunities to do good
  C. The rule is to be considered in all decisions
    1. How will this decision affect others?
    2. Is this what I would want someone else to do?

## Conclusion:

Do justice toward your brother, and you will come to love him; do injustice to him because you don't love him, and you will come to hate him. A Gospel of love for men with no prior love for God is a Gospel without life; a Gospel of love for God with no practical love for man, is a Gospel that is not genuine. Be sure you have the real thing.

# Obedience

## Matthew 7:24-29

**Introduction:**

Someone has said that obedience is, "Doing exactly what one is told to do when one is told to do it, with a good sprit." Children fail on this with parents, and believers likewise fail with God.

**I.  Obedience Is Difficult**
- A.  Because of certain implications
    1.  It implies that someone is out there
    2.  It implies that someone has authority
    3.  It implies that someone can tell me what to do
    4.  It implies that I can't do what I want
- B.  This is the heart of problem in Eden (Genesis 3:1-7)
    1.  "I'll do it my way"
    2.  Obedience disallows this

**II.  Obedience Is Demanded**
- A.  It has the highest priority. It is:
    1.  Worship (1 Samuel 15:22)
    2.  Religious observance (Isaiah)
    3.  Giving (Micah 6:7 & 8)
- B.  It is essential to the God-man relationship
    1.  The superiority of God
    2.  The glory of god
    3.  The wisdom of God

**III.  Obedience Is Decisive**
- A.  The points of the parable
    1.  Both men build houses
    2.  Both houses undergo storm
    3.  One passed; one failed
- B.  The points of difference
    1.  Both men heard the Word
    2.  The differences are in obedience
    3.  This explains much Christian success and failure

**Conclusion:**

We must recognize Someone worthy of obedience. God demands obedience. Our spiritual success or failure depends on it.

# Gratitude
### Luke 17:11-19

**Introduction:**
The recorded miracle isn't the main point of this passage. Such a fact is frequently true. The surrounding matters are significant. This miracle stresses gratitude by contrasting it with ingratitude.

I. **It is a typical story**
   - A. One out of ten returns to say "thanks"
   - B. It is tragically true that
     1. Many more pray than ever praise
     2. Many more receive than ever give
     3. Many more participate in ritual than ever really worship
   - C. It is a practical truth for today
     1. Many prayer requests; few praise items
     2. We take most of our blessings for granted

II. **It is a teaching story**
   - A. It teaches the characteristics of praise
     1. Individual—just one
     2. Prompt—he didn't complete his trip to the priest. That could wait
     3. Spiritual—it glorifies God
     4. Intense—note his loud voice
     5. Humble—We fell at His feet
     6. Focused—He didn't answer Christ's question
   - B. It teaches the benefits of praise
     1. It is right
     2. It manifests love and gratitude
     3. It is acceptable to Him
     4. It receives larger blessing

III. **It is a tempering story**
   - A. It encourages us when we are dealing with poor results
     1. He healed ten of leprosy and could only get thanks from one
     2. We win many to Christ and see few develop
   - B. It encourages us in the face of ingratitude
     1. Only one stopped to thank Him
     2. We must not allow such responses to discourage us

IV. **It is a testing story**
   - A. It tests our view of God's goodness
     1. He has done something better for us

2. How is our gratitude?
B. It tests our response to that goodness
   1. We claim to be grateful
   2. How is that gratitude shown?

## Conclusion:

This story shows us the human heart. We must be sure we don't do the same thing. How grateful are you? How is your gratitude showing?

# *Freedom*
### John 8:31-37

**Introduction:**

Our world has seen much of freedom in recent years. Very few people, however, really are free. Most live in bondage of one form or another to such things as:

I. **Guilt**
  A. Regret over things done or not done
  B. A nagging sense of failure
  C. Continuous discomfort

II. **Self**
  A. Prevalent questions and comments reveal modern man's condition
    1. "How does this affect me?"
    2. "What's in it for me?"
    3. "I just feel I should . . ."
    4. "No one tells me what to do"
  B. This is a most significant factor in our society

III. **Thinking and Emotions**
  A. Scrambled wires
    1. We know that feelings follow actions
    2. We live by the idea that actions follow emotions
    3. We become completely scrambled
  B. Remember the awesome power of biblical thinking

IV. **Passion**
  A. This moves beyond emotions (actually imbedded emotional patterns)
  B. Complusive behaviors
    1. Habits
    2. Desires
    3. Activities
  C. Is it true that we can't help ourselves?

V. **Sin**
  A. This deals in the realm of power
  B. There are two categories
    1. Things I know to be sin
    2. Things I don't know about but still are sin

VI. **Fear**
  A. There are three main focuses to fear:

1. God
2. Death
3. Punishment
B. There is much more of this in our world than there appears to be

**Conclusion:**

There are various ways out of these bondages, but only God delivers from them. Are you finding freedom from Him?

# Sanctification

## John 17:17

**Introduction:**

There is much controversy about this theme. The controversy concerns what it means, how it happens, and its extent. It is important to know its exact meaning.

I.   **The Meaning of Sanctification**
    A.  To make holy
    B.  To set apart
    C.  Illustrated: take a person or thing out of a group and put it aside

II.  **The Modes of Sanctification**
    A.  Positional—at time of conversion (1 Corinthians 1:30) - past tense
    B.  Progressive—throughout life (1 Thessalonians 4:3) - progressive tense
    C.  Perfect—ultimately in glory (1 John 3:2) - future tense

III. **The Manner of Sanctification**
    A.  Separation
        1.  From sin, world, lust, etc.
        2.  To likeness to Christ
    B.  It involves:
        1.  Cleansing
        2.  Dedication to God

IV.  **The Means of Sanctification**
    A.  The Holy Spirit
    B.  He uses the Word of God (John 17:17)
        1.  It is not used in any magical manner
        2.  We don't "claim by faith" when it comes to sanctification

V.   **The Mandate of Sanctification**
    A.  To get as near being like Christ as is possible
    B.  This is how to hear "well done"

**Conclusion:**

Holiness is not something to be dreaded. Being set apart makes us special. It is a very important concept (Hebrews 12:14). Are you sanctified? Are you being sanctified (at His pace)? If not, you will have a long way to go when you see Him.

# Encouragement
### John 21:1-11

**Introduction:**

The first and last miracles recorded in John are interesting. Both are gratuitous in that neither is in answer to any particular need. This miracle likely was done for its effect on the disciples. It was designed specifically to encourage them. It provides encouragement in five areas.

I. **Encouragement in Confusion**
   A. This was a "limbo" interim for them
   B. They decided to do what they knew, go fishing
   C. Christ blessed them in their doing
   D. It teaches us: when you don't know what to do, do what you know to do

II. **Encouragement in Labor**
   A. They had toiled long without results
      1. They were doing their own bidding
      2. They were surely disillusioned
   B. The results did come
      1. They kept on toiling
      2. He gave the results, counted abundance
   C. It teaches us: Keep on laboring in service; the results will come sooner or later

III. **Encouragement in Need**
   A. They were empty
      1. Likely wet and cold
      2. They had eaten nothing
   B. He made provision for them
      1. The provision came from His resources
      2. It was an abundant provision
      3. It was an unlimited provision when their fish were added in
   C. It teaches us: He knows our need (observes from the shore); He will come in the time of need; and His provision will be adequate

IV. **Encouragement in Priorities**
   A. They now had a huge catch
      1. They were commercial fisherman
      2. Something had to be done with the catch
   B. He made them come to breakfast
      1. They needed stamina for what was coming

2. Jesus teaches further after the meal
C. Teaching: "You will find it very hungry work if you try to live on catching and counting without being with Him." Your ability to feed others much depends on your dining with Him

## V. Encouragement in Failure
A. They all had performed poorly at the time of the crucifixion
 1. Doubt—Thomas
 2. Denial—Peter
 3. Departure—the rest
B. This was a time of healing
 1. It was provided by Him (He does all the preparation and serving)
 2. He dealt in restoration
C. Teaches: No matter what the failure, He is willing and anxious for restoration

## Conclusion:
Christ did a miracle of encouragement here. He spoke to their (and our) confusion, labor, need, priority systems, and failure. He wants to speak to us today. Will you hear Him? Will you heed Him?

# Our Inheritance

## Romans 8:17

**Introduction:**

Have you ever inherited any money (or thought you would)? Do you have a will? If the answer to either is yes, then you are familiar with this subject.

I. **The Inheritance**
   A. Its content:
      1. Seeing Him and enjoying His fellowship
      2. The glories of heaven
      3. Reigning with Him (Revelation 3:21)
      4. New things: body, name, etc.
   B. Its character (1 Peter 1:4)
      1. "Incorruptible"—imperishable
      2. "Undefiled"—unspoilable
      3. "Fadeth not away"—perennial
   C. Its comfort
      1. It is reserved in heaven
      2. We have a foretaste now
      3. All of creation will experience it (vs. 21)

II. **The One Who Bequeaths**
   A. The focus is on God
   B. The facts
      1. He cannot lie—it is absolutely sure
      2. He never dies—He oversees fully
      3. He can supply—He can produce what He has promised
      4. He has no needs—it won't run out
      5. He is equitable—it can't be unfair

III. **The Heirs**
   A. "Children" of God—a family relationship
   B. "Joint heirs"
      1. The inheritance is actually Christ's
      2. We are "in Him"
      3. Thus we have our inheritance because of our relationship to Him
   C. Proven children
      1. By suffering with Him
      2. Suffering that is "for" Him (or in connection with Him)
      3. Such suffering proves sonship

**Conclusion:**

This gives us a confident expectation of the future. This makes our current suffering and trials to endure and handle. This takes the abrasion out of the inequities of life. This gives us something worthwhile to aim at in the future. What does our inheritance mean to you?

Martin Luther had it right when he said:

"Riches are the pettiest and least worthy gifts which God can give a man. What are they to God's Word, to bodily gifts, such as beauty and health; or to the gifts of the mind, such as understanding, skill, wisdom! Yet men toil for them day and night, and take no rest. Therefore God commonly gives riches to foolish people to whom he gives nothing else."

# *Self*

Romans 12:3

**Introduction:**
Currently, there is a tremendous stress on self-concept. A good self-concept is seen as crucial. A poor self-concept is identified as the cause of most problems. Some teaching goes to foolish extremes, such as the idea that you have to love yourself before you can love others.

I. **The Great Deflation**
   A. Romans 12:3
      1. This is actually a caution against inflated self
      2. Be careful of turning it around
   B. Matthew 19:19
      1. This is a statement of command
      2. It means, "As you already love yourself"
   C. Ephesians 5:29
      1. Self-love is really normal
      2. Suicide is often the ultimate expression of excessive self-concept
   D. The facts of the matter
      1. The Bible doesn't condemn low self-esteem
      2. It does condemn pride about fifty times

II. **The Tell-Tale Signs of Pride**
   A. Unwillingness to accept correction
   B. Refusal to submit to authority
   C. Failure to obey the Word of God
   D. Tendency to excuse or rename sin
   E. Refusal to confront those who have wronged us
   F. Super-sensitivity
   G. Focus on self

III. **The Self-Imposed Sacrifice**
   A. It keeps us from claiming what we have in Christ by telling us that
      1. We can't be what we should be
      2. We can't do what we should do
      3. We can't have what we need to have
   B. It deflects obedience
      1. It makes obedience conditional
      2. It stresses conditions
      3. It excuses disobedience
   C. It prevents us from securing relief from wrong

1. Sin is dealt with by
   a. Admitting that something is sin
   b. Admitting that sin is wrong
   c. Seeking God's forgiveness
2. Our preoccupation with self-concept won't let us do these necessary things

**Conclusion:**

Who are you? You are a sinner saved by grace. Everything you are and have is related to the Savior. In Him, you have infinite worth. In yourself, you are nothing special. Why are you allowing your overblown self-concept to mess up in your life?

# Carnality

## 1 Corinthians 3:1-23

**Introduction:**
Expatriates are citizens who live in a foreign country. They must determine which way they will go on many issues. This is very similar to Christians in this world. Similar decisions must be made.

I.  **The Sickness**
    A.  Carnality = worldiness
    B.  What is worldliness?
        1.  The usual definition: things on a list of do's and don'ts
        2.  Actually it is a matter of orientation
            a.  We live in two realms (expatriates)
            b.  Worldliness is orientation to the old man and the natural world
    C.  Worldiness is an orientation that causes us to do things, rather than the things we do or don't do

II. **The Symptoms**
    A.  Inability to handle differences (3)
        1.  In the material realm—jealousy
        2.  In the interpersonal realm (4-8)
    B.  Preferring men (4-8)
        1.  One man over another
        2.  The most common form is that we shop for opinions rather than dig into the Word
    C.  Building with wrong materials (9-15)
        1.  Note various ingredients
            a.  Gold, etc. = spiritual things
            b.  Wood, etc. = worldly things
        2.  This likely deals with:
            a.  Biblical reality versus worldly reality
            b.  It is a matter of motives
    D.  Failure to appreciate the Holy Spirit (16 & 17)
        1.  This passage has reference to the church
        2.  Great care should be taken in the church
    E.  Confidence in human wisdom (18-23)
        1.  Personal opinions are placed before God's opinions
        2.  This is accepting the world's wisdom over God's

III. **The Source**
    A.  Which came first (1 & 2)
        1.  Biblical ignorance?
        2.  Shallowness?

B. The truth
   1. We are worldly because we are biblically shallow
   2. We are biblically shallow because we are worldly

## IV. The Solution
A. The answer lies in a decision of the will
   1. We live in two societies
   2. We must decide which one will dominate
B. This is what 1 John 2:15 means

## Conclusion:

All of us are worldly in some ways. Have you determined which way you are going to lean and live? Carnality (worldliness) is a problem of major proportion in today's church. Are you part of the problem? Are you part of the solution?

# *Judgment*

## 1 Corinthians 4:1-8

**Introduction:**

We often do poorly at the things we are required to do and do well at the things we are forbidden to do. Such is the case in this passage.

I.  **A Significant Difference**
   A.  We are commanded to be discerning, to make differences on the basis of objective and visible evidence (1 Corinthians 2:14; 12:10)
   B.  We are forbidden to judge, to form opinions about, to criticize, to censure (Matthew 7:1 & 2; Luke 6:37; Romans 14:10,13)

II. **A Clear Command**
   A.  It is simply stated—"judge nothing"
   B.  It has to do with passing judgment on invisible or non-objective matters
   C.  In short it says, "stay off the throne and the judicial bench"

III. **A List of Reasons**
   A.  Because other men ultimately are solely accountable to God (1)
       1.  Paul sees himself thus
       2.  He was a servant, belonging to Christ, who was given his ministry
   B.  Because we use incorrect criteria (2)
       1.  Faithfulness is the prime criteria
       2.  We tend to use various others
   C.  Because we can't judge ourselves (3 & 4)
       1.  Christ is the Lord of our conscience; only He can judge it justly
       2.  A clear conscience is significant but not finally determinative
   D.  Because there is an appointed time of judgment coming (5b)
       1.  God will judge unseen things
       2.  There is a proper time and place
       3.  Our judgment usurps God's throne
   E.  Because only God can know the things that we can't (5c)
       1.  He will expose what is hidden in the darkness
       2.  This is basically the motives, etc., of the human heart
   F.  Because we don't qualify as judges (6-8)

1. We don't understand the necessary factors
2. We don't have the necessary wisdom
3. We uniformly do a poor job

**Conclusion:**

We need more discernment; we need less judgment. We can't know what others think and feel, so we should identify our judgments as such. Are you doing poorly at what you should do? Are you doing well at what you are forbidden to do?

# Legal Problems
## 1 Corinthians 6:1-8

**Introduction:**

Sometimes an apparent problem covers a more serious problem. Sometimes an apparent problem covers the real problem. The surface problem here is serious, but the worst part of it is that it covers other problems and disguises the real problem.

I.  **The Apparent Problem (1)**
    A.  Stated: believers going to law before unbelievers
    B.  Explained:
        1.  This has to do with civil matters
        2.  This is an appeal, not a command
        3.  This does not relate to unbelievers

II. **The Additional Problems (2-8)**
    A.  A wrong view of the church (2 & 3)
        1.  God trusts saints
        2.  Saints are special—they will judge mankind and angels
        3.  Christians don't trust church structure for solving problems
    B.  A wrong attitude (4)
        1.  The things dealt with here could be judged by the least in the church
        2.  This shows the relative unimportance of such matters
        3.  They were making unimportant things greatly important
    C.  A wrong approach (5)
        1.  Are there no wise among you?
        2.  Are all the wise in the world?
        3.  Christians are actually wiser than unbelievers
    D.  Wrong values (6)
        1.  They were going to law before unbelievers
        2.  This resulted in:
            a.  Showing their problems to the whole world
            b.  Admitting their incompetence
            c.  Compromising their beliefs
        3.  There must be a concern with testimony
    E.  A wrong spirit (7)
        1.  Why do you not rather take wrong?
        2.  Subsidiary questions
            a.  Why not be like Christ?
            b.  Are things really that important?
        3.  You are all tied up in your own rights

F. Wrong actions
   1. You do the kinds of things that result in going to law
   2. It's wrong to do these things and worse to do them to brethren

## III. The Actual Problems
A. Stated: materialistic humanism—humanistic materialism
   1. Materialism: preoccupation with possession, ownership, rights
   2. Humanism: preoccupation with appearances and human wisdom
B. Going to law showed that there was something wrong underneath
C. They needed to deal with the real problem

**Conclusion:**
We've learned not to go to court against fellow believers, but have we learned to deal with the real problems that drive us to court?

- Our low view of the church and of its ability to deal with problems
- Our materialistic mentality that makes things more important than people
- Our humanism that places unlimited faith in human wisdom

If we would make the local church the court of last resort, we might be too embarrassed to pursue materialsim and humanism, our real problems.

# Immorality

## 1 Corinthians 6:9-20

### Introduction:

All sin is sin, but the Bible seems to view some sin more serious-ly. Murder usurps the authority of God. Immorality is also heavily condemned. This passage teaches against immorality and gives five reasons why it is so bad.

I. **Because It Confuses Our Identity (9-11)**
   A. It reveals the absence of the change that accompanies salvation
   B. It identifies us with the wrong crowd
   C. It misunderstands the work of conversion
      1. You did such "things"
      2. But something happened

II. **Because It Violates God's Order (12)**
   A. We are not always completely able to control our emotions
   B. We are responsible to control our actions
   C. Immorality is a matter of emotions controlling actions

III. **Because It Defies God's Purposes (13-17)**
   A. God's purposes for the body:
      1. It is temporary
      2. It is to be used for God's glory. We are more than responders to the animal impulse
      3. It belongs to Christ
   B. Immorality results in a union of bodies
      1. "He who joins himself" (16)
      2. It brings Christ into a wrong relationship
   C. Immorality creates a contradiction
      1. What belongs to Christ is offered to another
      2. The biblical picture is thus out of focus

IV. **Because It Is Sin Against One's Body (18)**
   A. It involves the body. Most sin doesn't
   B. It raises questions about the self
      1. Self-respect
      2. Ability to keep covenant
      3. Self-control
   C. Flee, keep on fleeing immorality. Some things, fight; immorality, flee

V. **Because It Misunderstands the Body's Role (19 & 20)**
   A. The Holy Spirit dwells in us

B. We are not our own
   1. The final determination of our body is not ours
   2. It changes all relationships and concepts
C. Our body should be used to glorify God

**Conclusion:**

There are two key directions here: "Keep on fleeing fornication," and,"Glorify God in your body." We are commanded not even to think about immorality. It is very difficult to live this way today. The commandments of God's Word never depend on the standards of any contemporary society. We need to make some heart commitments and then keep on fleeing.

# Love

## 1 Corinthians 13

**Introduction:**

1 Corinthians 13 is not isolated; it is part of a context. There must have been a big problem in Corinth regarding gifts note 12:31. The purpose of a this chapter: to point out the supremacy of love.

I. **The Importance of Love (1-3)**
   - A. Three illustrations are given
     1. Speaking with tongues is like clashing brass or cymbals without love
     2. The best gifts are meaningless without love
     3. Ultimate acts of self-sacrifice are of no value without love
   - B. No spiritual act has meaning without love. There is nothing I can do more important than love

II. **The Nature of Love (4-7)**
   - A. The qualities of love are listed
     1. Patient
     2. Kind
     3. Not jealous
     4. Not boastful
     5. Not proud
     6. Not rude
     7. Not self-centered
     8. Not easily angered
     9. Keeps no record of evil
     10. Rejoices not over wrong
     11. Rejoices with the truth
     12. All things covers (protects)
     13. All things believes
     14. All things hopes
     15. All things endures
   - B. This is different from the usual definition of love in that:
     1. It is non-emotional
     2. It is very active
     3. Is is a reasonable facsimile of the love God has for us

III. **The Endurance of Love (8-12)**
   - A. The main point is that love outlives all other spiritual gifts
   - B. At some point, prophecy, knowledge, and tongues will cease, but love never will

IV. **The Supremacy of Love (13)**

A. Gifts cease but concepts continue
   1. The gifts ultimately are not needed
   2. The concepts continue to be needed
B. Love is the greatest of the continuing concepts
   1. All are recognized as great
   2. If you can have only one, choose love

**Conclusion:**

Most of us know very little of real love. If you are seeking gifts, be sure of love first. Our greatest spiritual need is developing love to God and showing love to others. Don't concentrate on gifts; concentrate on love.

# Giving

## 1 Corinthians 16:1-4

**Introduction:**

This passage deals with a specific collection. It was for a need in the Jerusalem church, but we don't know why the need existed. In the process of taking the offering, Paul lays down some important principles regarding giving in general.

I. **Giving Should Be Regular**
   A. A regular basis: "first day of every week"
      1. It should be systematic
      2. Make it as easy on yourself as possible
   B. A matter of priority—"set aside"
      1. It should be before everything else
      2. It should be an exciting thing

II. **Giving Should Be Personal**
   A. "Let everyone of you"
      1. Each is to participate
      2. It is both a duty and a privilege
   B. "Each of you by himself"
      1. It doesn't depend on what others do
      2. It is between each man and his God
      3. The problem is that we often fail to consider God
   C. The misunderstanding
      1. We should not let others know
         a. So our reward will not be lost
         b. So our pride will not be built
      2. We should not be ashamed of letting others know

III. **Giving Should Be Relational**
   A. Principle: proportional
   B. Practical truths
      1. God gives to us that we may give to others
      2. Prosperity should create greater giving, and greater giving will create prosperity
   C. Basic recognitions are required
      1. Where it all comes from
      2. How God sees things

IV. **Giving Is a Planned Matter**
   A. Paul didn't want to collect when he was present
      1. Likely not because of a natural aversion
      2. Likely more a matter of wanting them to plan ahead
   B. The presentation of needs

1. Giving should be based on principle, not on needs, appeals, etc.
2. The presentation of need is not wrong, but it should not be necessary

## V. Giving Is a Matter of Liberality
A. Note Paul's mention of other churches
1. He is seeking to spur, not shame
2. He says, "If you are really as good as you think, you will show it"
B. We ought to be trying to surpass ourselves
1. We should be giving to genuine causes
2. "Self-denial and liberality were among the distinguishing virtues of the early Christians," and they go together

## Conclusion:

Most ministries would struggle far less if all God's people would plug into the biblical pattern. Individuals would struggle far less that way also. Where are you, relative to your giving?

# Zeal

## Galatians 4:12-18

**Introduction:**

Christ was consumed by zeal. One of the disciples was called, "The Zealot." There was a Zealot political party. Paul says it is a good thing to be zealous. "Zeal" comes from the word for "boiling." It means to bubble up, to be stirred. Paul says it is a good thing to be zealously affected. Why?

**I.  Because It Benefits the Individual (Galatians 4:12-18)**
   A.  The Galatians had been very zealous, but their zeal had flagged
   B.  In their loss of zeal, they had lost:
      1.  Their joy ("where is then the blessedness?")
      2.  Their doctrinal purity (17)
      3.  Their self-motivation (18b)
   C.  The benefits of zeal:
      1.  It keeps the fire burning
      2.  It keeps the "motor" running
      3.  It keeps the joybells ringing

**II.  Because It Fulfills Our Purpose (Titus 2:11-15)**
   A.  God desires to do something special with His people
   B.  God's purposes involve:
      1.  A "peculiar" people
      2.  A people "zealous of good works"
   C.  We can't fulfill God's purposes without zeal for good works

**III.  Because It Is Pleasing to God (Revelation 3:14-19)**
   A.  The Laodicean church was condemned for its lukewarmness
   B.  God is displeased by:
      1.  Lukewarmness
      2.  People who have problems and don't know they have them
   C.  The answer to lukewarmness is
      1.  Repentance
      2.  Zeal

**Conclusion:**

We are casual Christians. We suffer personal loss. We fail to fulfill the purpose for which we were designed. We run the risk of divine judgment. God wants us on fire. Isn't it time to light a match?

# The Laws of the Harvest

## Galatians 6:7

**Introduction:**

Farming is a mystery to many of us. There are, however, some things we all know. We know the difference between a chicken, a pig, a cow, etc. We also know the laws of harvest: You must sow to reap. You normally reap what you sow. You normally reap more than you sow. You normally reap sometime after you sow. The Bible has its own laws of the harvest which are worth examining.

I.   **Sowing and Reaping Are Inescapable (Romans 2:6-10)**
    A. This is different from nature
        1. "No sow, no reap"
        2. We reap what wasn't sown
    B. Sowing is inescapable
        1. We do not choose to sow, we do sow
        2. The only question is what we sow
    C. Reaping is sure
        1. Sometimes we lose a harvest naturally
        2. We never do so spiritually
    D. Only repentance breaks the chain of sowing and reaping
        1. This deals with evil and its consequences
        2. We may escape consequences, but we will not escape final responsibility

II.  **Sowing and Reaping Are Relational**
    A. We reap in kind
        1. Evil produces evil
        2. Good produces good
    B. Reaping follows a natural law
        1. You get out what you put in
        2. Usually, sowing and reaping are directly related
            a. Caution: you may not get what you expect. Reaping may not be limited to you
            b. This was illustrated in David. How awful to see the reaping in the lives of our children
    C. Reaping is in proportion (2 Corinthians 9:6)
        1. It is usually directly related
        2. You only get out what you put in
    D. Reaping is often more than what is sown (Luke 6:38)
        1. God determines proportions
        2. The reaping may involve some work on our part

III. **Sowing and Reaping Are Sequential (Galatians 6:9)**

A. Sowing and reaping are often separated by time
   1. We don't get weary from work but rather from lack of success
   2. Notice:
      a. "Be not weary," not "don't quit"
      b. "In" well-doing—don't stop
      c. "Due season"—His timing
B. God cares for the sow-reap interval
   1. Hebrews 6:10
   2. The ultimate results are up to Him
C. Stay on the farm until the time of reaping
   1. Hebrews 10:36
   2. We are not even to get tired
D. We can't escape negative reaping as God oversees the interval

## Conclusion:

You are sowing what? You will reap what? Have you resigned because of lack of fruit? You need to re-examine. Are you going to be satisfied with the harvest?

# The Cross

## Galatians 6:14

**Introduction:**

Many churches paint their doors red as a symbol of the fact that the way into the church is through the blood of Christ. This is just one of many symbols. The most prominent symbol, however, is the cross. It is frequently seen, and it stands for Christ's death on the cross.

I.  **The Centrality of the Cross in Christianity**
    A.  It is shown in this passage
        1.  False teachers were glorying in what they were getting people to do, to obey their false teaching
        2.  Paul strikes a contrast with them in that he will glory in nothing but the cross
    B.  It is supported by other passages
        1.  The apex of the preaching of Paul (1 Corinthians 2:2)
        2.  The basis of the preaching of Paul (1 Corinthians 1:22 & 23)
        3.  The impetus of the ministry of Paul (Philippians 3:10)

II. **The Centrality of the Cross in Salvation**
    A.  The cross is the only means of salvation
        1.  Paul says, "by whom (which) the world is crucified unto me," which means that anything else that might be trusted for salvation is dead
        2.  This includes the law, works, church membership, giving, self, etc.
        3.  All the things I might trust for salvation are rendered dead by the cross of Christ
    B.  The cross is the only means of effecting a change in life
        1.  Paul says, "and I unto the world"
            a.  Not only is the world dead for me, but I am dead in so far as the world is concerned
            b.  This means that a radical break has come
        2.  This is backed by verse 15
            a.  No works or efforts can avail
            b.  Salvation involves a new creation which only comes about through the cross

III. **The Centrality of the Cross in Sanctification**
    A.  Explanation
        1.  When we are saved through faith in the cross, we become possessed with a new standing before God

2. When we are possessed with a new standing before God, we are challenged to bring life into conformity to that new standing

B. The cross is central in sanctification because, through it, the appeal of the world is broken ("By which the world is crucified unto me")

1. The world should not be trusted in to provide anything even though it is often trusted for such things as security, entertainment, satisfaction, and security

2. Many Christians are frustrated because they are trusting in the world

## Conclusion:

Until we see the centrality of the cross, we will not find salvation, and we are not likely to progress in sanctification.

# Redemption

## Ephesians 1:7

**Introduction:**

There are many blessings mentioned in this context. Among them are election, predestination, adoption, and acceptance in the Beloved. Another of these great spiritual blessings is in verse 7. It is redemption.

I. **Its Nature**
   A. Its definition: setting free a person or thing that has come to belong to another
   B. Its illustration is in Leviticus 25:47-49
   C. Its explanation
      1. "Redemption" descibes the act of God by which He sets sinners free
      2. It is bound up with salvation but technically separate from it
      3. It is a term that is frequently used but little understood

II. **Its Method**
   A. Man belonged to God by creation but was taken by Satan because of sin
   B. In order for man to be set free, sin must be paid off
   C. Only blood can pay for sin
      1. Why? Because the Bible says so in Hebrews 9:22
      2. This is to show that sin could not be treated lightly
      3. The blood represents the death of Christ here
   D. The blood of Christ insures this redemption
      1. He gave His life and all that He had for sin
      2. Sin has been paid for

III. **Its Price**
   A. Christ gave His life to secure this
   B. We stand in awe of a God who would pay a price such as this

IV. **Its Benefits**
   A. Redemption is a setting free
      1. From sin, Satan, and bondage
      2. To Christ and new life
   B. Forgiveness is not just another name for redemption

V. **Its Source**
   A. The negative side: it is not just through or by Him
   B. The positive side

1. It is through union with Him
2. Salvation is in His Person
C. Applied—Have you been joined to Christ?

**Conclusion:**

Redemption is more than a fancy theological concept. It is the work of God whereby I can be bought back from Satan. It is secured through trusting Christ.

# Grace

## Ephesians 1:7 & 8

**Introduction:**

What would you do if you inherited a million dollars? Don't be too sure it won't happen; you have the world's richest Father. In reality, however, most of His wealth is in things like grace.

I. **The Riches of His Grace**
   A. "Grace" comes to equal all spiritual blessings wrapped up in salvation
   B. "Riches"
      1. There is tremendous wealth here
      2. This wealth is shown in the forgiveness of sins

II. **The Riches Demonstrated**
   A. In forgiveness
   B. In His abounding toward us in all wisdom and prudence
      1. He has overflowed in "wisdom": that which God imparts to the individual so he can know what is right and wrong
      2. He has overflowed in "prudence": the insight and intelligence given to enable us to do what wisdom tells us is right.
   C. In His abounding "toward us"

III. **The Extent of the Abounding**
   A. "He hath abounded"
      1. Notice the past perfect tense which speaks of something already accomplished
      2. When did He abound?
         a. Not at the cross. That was just where His love was shown
         b. Not at conversion. That was just where we came to know it
         c. Actually from eternity past. A great reservoir of grace has existed since before time began
   B. Grace abounds even to the chief of sinners
      1. Grace is there and available to all who will receive it
      2. The benefits of grace, wisdom and prudence are also available to all who know His grace

**Conclusion:**

God has abounded toward you. He has poured out His grace to you in an abundant manner. Have you responded to His grace?

# Righteousness

## Philippians 2:12 & 13

**Introduction:**

This is a somewhat confusing passage. Most of the confusion comes because people choose to get confused. We think, "I don't understand; therefore, I am not responsible for action." Actually, this confusing passage is easy to understand but hard to act upon.

I. **The Meaning**
- A. A Possible Explanation
    1. The overall problem in the book was one of division (4:2)
    2. This section deals with that problem
    3. A suggested translation, "Work out your own solution"
- B. A Preferred Explanation
    1. "Salvation" has several meanings
    2. Work out the salvation you already know in the general course of life
    3. Ephesians 2:8-10 is a commentary on this passage

II. **The Message**
- A. Work out
    1. Develop
    2. Allow to work out
- B. Salvation
    1. The implications of your salvation
    2. Make your salvation practical

III. **The Method**
- A. Freedom
    1. From fear, death, hell, future, unknown, etc.
    2. From self-effort - no longer at all responsible for our own salvation (we never were, but we now know it)
    3. From being dominated by emotions, others, Satan
- B. Responsibility
    1. To discern the will of God. The Word of God is the best source of this
    2. To do the commands of God. All His commands designed to be done
    3. To properly represent God
- C. Opportunity
    1. To show designed fulfillment of humanity
        a. No man can ever reach what he was supposed to have been

          b.  The Christian can come the closest
     2.  To explore the riches of your full potential
          a.  You can become what you are supposed to be
          b.  We have the possibility of being far more through answered prayer
     3.  To lay up eternal treasure
          a.  No one else can do lasting things
          b.  We have access to eternity

**IV.  The Manner**
    A.  With fear and trembling
       1.  A fear of God and His power
       2.  A trembling toward sin and its ability
    B.  It is God that worketh within you
       1.  He shows His will
       2.  He enables us to do what we have been shown

**Conclusion:**
Salvation has incredible implications. We have seen just a very few. They keep on going. "Work out your own salvation," is a commandment. What are you doing in this regard? What should you be doing?

# Spiritual Strength

## Philippians 4:13

**Introduction:**
We live in negative world. We are more acquainted with negatives than with positives. We don't have, we can't do, and we didn't get. The Bible sounds a needed positive message in this passage.

I. **It Is Personal—"I"**
   A. We generalize truth
   B. We need to personalize. This pertains to me personally

II. **It Is Positive—"Can"**
   A. This contrasts with negative Christianity
   B. This stresses enormous potential
      1. Most never dream of their possibilities
      2. As a result, most never touch what they could

III. **It Is Practical—"Do"**
   A. This has to do with actual living. It refers to very specific things
   B. This gets the Bible off the page and into life

IV. **It Is Pervasive—"All things"**
   A. It is obviously limited
   B. "I can do all things that I am required or expected to do"
      1. I can endure all trials
      2. I can perform all duties
      3. I can obey all commandments
      4. I can perform all service effectively
      5. I can overcome all internal spiritual conflicts
      6. I can face every crisis
   C. This is a simple statement of fact that could change our lives if we really believed it

V. **It Is Providential—"Through Christ"**
   A. This brings in the divine dimension
   B. This sets the perimeters
      1. The things Christ is concerned with
      2. The things Christ will be associated with
      3. The things I can ask Christ to bless
   C. This establishes my dependency. I don't do it alone

VI. **It Is Powerful—"Which Strengtheneth Me"**
   A. He is the source of my power
      1. He, not I, makes it possible

2. I must draw on the source
B. He provides that which I need
   1. It comes from Him
   2. He knows what I need
   3. He gives it to me as I need it

**Conclusion:**

This is a great encouragement when in trial, overwhelmed by duty, burdened by a commandment, staggered by requirements of service, torn with conflict, or facing crisis. This is a bedrock basic. You must get Christ's strength in order to do anything and everything in the Christian life.

# Hope

### Colossians 1:27

**Introduction:**

We say, "I hope so," and thus we designate desire. When the Bible says, "I hope so," it designates certainty.

I. **What Is Hope?**
   A. It is confident expectation
   B. It is confident expectation regarding the unseen and the future
   C. It is confident expectation based on fact

II. **What Is Hope Based On?**
   A. That God will continue being what He has always been (2 Timothy 2:13)
   B. That God will successfully complete whatever He has begun (Philippians 1:6)
   C. That God will keep all His promises (2 Corinthians 1:20)
   D. That Christ will come again as He has promised (2 Peter 3:4-12)
   E. That there will be complete justice and equity established (Romans 14:10; Hebrews 9:27)

III. **What Does Hope Produce? (Great to have this kind of hope)**
   A. Joyful confidence in God (Romans 8:28, 12:12)
   B. An anchor amidst the storms of life (Hebrews 6:18 & 19; 1 Thessalonians 4:13)
   C. Endurance under trial (Romans 5:3; 1 Thessalonians 1:3)
   D. Perseverance in prayer (1 Thessalonians 5:17)
   E. Purifying power (1 John 3:3)

**Conclusion:**

Our lives are filled with unknowns. We need hope, confident expectation. Is hope accomplishing its work in you? If not, what's wrong?

# Good Works

## 2 Thessalonians 3:13

**Introduction:**

These are needy times—internationally, nationally, personally, and ecclesiastically. Paul provides a needed word for this needy world.

I. **What Is Well Doing?**
   A. The common tasks of everyday life (if not "well doing" then don't do them)
   B. Meeting the needs of others
   C. Obeying the Word of God
   D. Serving the Lord
   E. Summary: Doing what I believe and know to be right

II. **Why Do We Grow Weary in Doing It?**
   A. Because of unworthy, ungrateful recipients
   B. Because of the idleness of others
   C. Because of unreasonable and wicked men
   D. Because of critics and busybodies
   E. Because of the lack of results and progress
   F. Because of a general personal spiritual decline

III. **What Are the Facts?**
   A. Well doing requires effort
   B. Well doing requires self-denial
   C. Well doing may bring problems
   D. Well doing requires a narrow focus (not on what others do or don't do)
   E. Well doing can't be based on results
   F. Summary: well doing costs us something

IV. **Why Should We Worry About Well Doing?**
   A. Because it is a commandment
   B. Notice what is commanded:
      1. We are not prohibited from quitting
      2. We are prohibited from even growing weary
   C. Weariness in well doing is both disobedient and sin

V. **How Can We Avoide Growing Weary?**
   A. We must have a right focus
      1. Do right because it is right
      2. Do all we know to be right
   B. We must have a deep inner commitment
   C. We must have a valid walk with the Lord

D.  We must understand the nature of Christianity

**Conclusion:**

In what have you grown weary? Has what was once right become wrong, or are you just tired of it? This is a needed word for a needy world because of what the world needs: People who do right, people who do right no matter what, people who keep on doing what is right no matter what.

# *Faith*

Hebrews 11:1-3

**Introduction:**

People believe strange things: reincarnation, astrology, occultism, pryamid power, healers, etc., and call them all "faith." How different from what the Bible says about faith

I. **Faith Is Believing**
   A. "The substance of things hoped for"
      1. "Substance," surety, being sure
      2. "Being sure of what we hope for"
   B. "The evidence of things not seen"
      1. "Evidence," certainty, being certain
      2. "Being certain of what we do not see"
   C. This is much more objective than usually admitted
      1. It is based on the idea of an unseen world
      2. It is based on knowledge, on fact rather than feeling because, "feelings are the enemy of faith"

II. **Faith Is Believing in God**
   A. It must be in someone or something to have meaning
      1. Much faith today is in faith itself
      2. Faith without basis is irrational
   B. Biblical faith is described in Hebrews 11:6b
      1. We must believe that God exists
      2. We must believe that He can and will do something ("Faith is not believing that God can, but that He will")
   C. Christian faith requires facts for meaning
      1. The Bible is not the only source of revelation
      2. The Bible is the only place that interprets revelation
      3. The Bible is absolutely necessary for meaningful Christian faith
      4. The Christian faith is the only meaningful religious faith

III. **Faith Is Believing in God Enough to Do Certain Things**
   A. Act on His promises
      1. They must be properly understood
      2. All else must be in order
      3. "If there are ways and means, there is no faith"
   B. Obey His commandments
      1. Often involves difficulty
         a. They run counter to our thinking
         b. They go against our desires
         c. They create discomfort

       2. Faith can act because it believes that God knows what is best

       3. Faith is the issue in much disobedience

C. Accept His Word

       1. God is very clear on this

          a. "Without faith . . . (Hebrew 11:6)

          b. ". . . not of works" (Ephesians 2:9)

          c. "Except a man . . ." (John 3:3)

       2. There is no salvation without faith and no faith without accepting His Word

       3. Salvation is secured God's way or not at all

**Conclusion:**

Christianity is sometimes presented as "pie in the sky by and by." Actually, Christianity is belief in the existence, ability and willingness of God to the point that one lives by His promises, obeys His commands and accepts His Word as final on any matter.

# *Praise*
## Hebrews 13:15 & 16

**Introduction:**

One reason I'm glad I didn't live in Old Testament times is my disinterest in slaughtering animals. I'm glad that the sacrificial system ended. But has it really ended? We still have an obligation to a particular sacrifice.

I.   **It is to be a continuous sacrifice**
- A.   Its conditions
  1. At all times
  2. In all situations
  3. Under all circumstances
  4. In all mind-frames
- B.   A commandment to all God's people
- C.   We must cultivate perpetual gratitude ("Pray without ceasing" elsewhere; "Praise without ceasing" here)

II.   **It is to be a costly sacrifice**
- A.   It will involve effort
  1. Creativity
  2. Concentration
- B.   It will divert energies
  1. When we would rather be complaining, we will praise
  2. Instead of what we would prefer to talk about, we will talk about what we should
  3. It takes attention away from self
- C.   Real involvement will cost some frustration as we realize we fall so far short

III.   **It is to be a communicated sacrifice**
- A.   It must be spoken as this text deals with spoken praise
- B.   It must be lived (vs. 16)
  1. It must be more than talk
  2. We can't always be talking, but we can always be praising
- C.   It must be natural
  1. "The fruit of the lips"
  2. Praise for the Christian is as natural as blasphemy for the profane
     a. It must be spoken to be meaningful
     b. It must be lived to be authentic
     c. It must be natural to be effective

IV.   **It is to be a consecrated sacrifice**

A. This becomes possible only as all that we are and have belong to Him
B. The requisite: how can we praise if we are continually railing at His providence and provision?
C. The greater the consecration, the more likely the sacrifice of praise

## Conclusion:

The Psalmist understood this concept and shows that fact in Psalm 116:12-17. The sin of failing to praise is not so serious as a violation of the moral law, but it is one far more frequently committed. Will you set your heart to learn the godly discipline of continual praise?